F

WAS A

FANCIFUL FROG

EDMUND DULAC'S LIMERICKS

Abbeville Press · Publishers · New York · London · Paris
In Association with The Library of Congress

Editor: Amy Handy
Designer: Molly Shields
Production supervisor: Matthew Pimm

Library of Congress Cataloging-in-Publication Data

Dulac, Edmund, 1882–1953.
[Lyrics, pathetic & humorous, from A to Z]
F was a fanciful frog : Edmund Dulac's limericks.
p.   cm.
Originally published: Lyrics, pathetic & humorous,
from A to Z.
London ; New York : F. Warne, 1908. With new introd.
Summary: An illustrated collection of limericks for each
letter of the alphabet, presenting humorous or odd charac-
ters from an Afghan Ameer to the old mathematician
who carries X, Y, and Z in his head.
ISBN 1-55859-640-2
1. Limericks. [1. Limericks. 2. English poetry.
3. Alphabet.]
I. Title.
PR6007.U46L9 1993   93-24777
821'.912–dc20   CIP
                                              AC

INTRODUCTION

The early twentieth century was a golden age of illustrated books, a time when exquisitely produced volumes unveiled fantastic dreams and exotic visions. Along with Arthur Rackham, Kay Nielsen, and W. Heath Robinson, one of the most eminent illustrators of the genre was Edmund Dulac.

Born in Toulouse, France, Dulac (1882–1953) originally studied law, but after several years' persistence as an art student he was able to pursue art as his chosen career. A devoted Anglophile deeply interested in book illustration, he was particularly inspired by the work of William Morris and Aubrey Beardsley. Shortly after emigrating to England in 1904 (he became a British subject in 1912), Dulac received a commission for his first set of book illustrations, a new edition of the Brontës' novels, to be published by J. M. Dent. His next important commission, for Leicester Galleries, was a set of watercolor illustrations of *The Arabian Nights.* Since Dulac had always been intrigued by Eastern traditions and by the sparkling color and rich patterns of Persian miniatures, this project proved a perfect vehicle for him and helped to assure his future as an illustrator. Not only a master draftsman and superb watercolorist, Dulac also designed costumes, furniture, bank notes, and stamps; composed music; and proved a capable writer. Today he is primarily remembered for the spectacular book illustrations he produced in the early part of his career, but all his creations demonstrate his extravagant originality and intense imaginativeness.

For this book, first published in 1908 by Frederick Warne, Dulac produced both the illustrations *and* the text. Ostensibly a children's alphabet in limerick form, the verses sometimes rely on surprisingly sophisticated vocabulary. And, very occasionally, the book resorts to phrasing that today would be considered objectionable or biased. But as the product of an earlier, less culturally enlightened era, the verses may give the reader a glimpse of the mores of the time. Also, American readers must bear in mind that the final verse depends upon British pronunciation—the letter "z" must be pronounced "zed" for the rhyme to succeed.

Most of the illustrations possess a lighthearted and enchanting simplicity. The charming endpapers probably owe something of their whimsy to Dulac's association with the London Sketch Club, where he had honed his skill for humorous drawing. Standing before newly lit candles, a jester begins a serenade: the merriment is about to commence. When the end of the alphabet is reached, the jester makes his exit, strolling past the burnt-out candles, his serenade—and Dulac's remarkable verses—now complete. Over the next half-century Dulac was to produce work of supreme inventiveness; this delightful volume was just the beginning.

Lyrics Pathetic and Humorous from A–Z, on which this volume is based, is one of 650,000 items in the Rare Book and Special Collections Division of the Library of Congress. Some 18,200 of these items are children's books dating from the early eighteenth century to the present.

The Library of Congress houses 100 million items, including books, manuscripts, graphic illustrations, prints, photographs, posters, music, sound recordings, film, and maps. In addition to serving Congress, the Library is also an important resource for scholars, researchers, artists, scientists, and the general public. Its universal collection represents virtually all cultures and languages of the world.

A was an Afghan Ameer
Who played the accordion by ear.
  When ambassadors called,
  They first listened appalled,
Then would suddenly all disappear.

B was a burly burgrave
Who boasted he bold was and brave.
But he blushed, it is said,
Till his beard turned quite red,
So he thought it were better to shave.

C was a cook from Chang-Chew
Who once made a crocodile stew.
   But when called by the bell,
   His red pepper-box fell,
So that all he could answer was "Tchew."

D was a dignified dame
Who doubtless was not much to blame.
  She played draughts with a lord,
  And was dreadfully bored,
Which occasioned the loss of her game.

E was an exquisite elf
Who enjoyed being quite by herself.
   She delighted to play
   In an elegant way
With the things that she found on a shelf.

F was a fanciful frog
Who stayed fifty years on a log;
For he never would spend
A night out with a friend,
As he feared to be lost in a fog.

G was a giddy young girl,
With a gaudy green hat and a curl.
She was not commonplace,
And displayed so much grace
While playing at golf with an earl.

H was a hard-headed hare
Who had such a horrible scare!
As he opened one day,
In the most heedless way,
A hamper marked "handle with care"!

I was an impudent imp
Who invited an over-cooked shrimp
  To a slide on the ice,
  As the weather was nice.
Next day the shrimp walked with a limp.

J was a juvenile Jap
Who met with a dreadful mishap;
For she bitterly cried,
When an insect she spied
On her flower, just taking a nap.

K was a kind-hearted King
Who once taught a bird how to sing,
By knocking a pan
With the knob of a fan,
And a kettle tied on to a string.

L was a Lorn little lass
With a grief that no grief could surpass.
John had left for the field
With his sword, lance, and shield,
And his luncheon inside his cuirass.

M was a merry milk-maid,
Who one morning was sadly dismayed;
For a mischievous mouse,
That Puss found in the house,
Was the cause of a slump in her trade.

N was a neat necromancer
Who once had a call from a dancer;
But he never let out
What she asked him about,
And a secret it made of his answer.

O was an obstinate owl
Who might have been quite a nice fowl;
But she spoilt her eye sight
Reading novels at night.
Now she ogles at you with a scowl.

P was a proud, pompous prince
Who lived on plum-pudding and quince.
Once he put by mistake
In his pipe a pancake,
And has been very pale ever since.

Q was a quaint dainty queen
Who once made a quilt for a dean,
With some quadruple tweeds,
Quite a number of beads,
And a queer little quill in between.

R was a rubicund rustic
Who wrote a romantic acrostic,
In which roses and thrushes,
And rabbits and rushes,
To the rhyme gave a flavour agrestic.

S was a short-sighted squire
Who solemnly sang in a choir;
    And he passed from staccato
    To a soft moderato
In a fashion that all did admire.

T was a tragical traitor
Who had more than one imitator.
As he totally thrived
On the gifts he derived
From the hands of the tender spectator.

U was a youthful Undine
In the kingdom of ultramarine.
Often week after week
She would play hide and seek,
In the weeds with an ugly sardine.

V was a virtuous vicar
   Who played on the violin with vigour,
     It was easy to see
     The variation in **C**
   Had not vainly been marked "a bit quicker."

What was the W then?
A whale, a wee worm, or a wren?
Or a witch of the wood
With a wonderful hood,
Who winked at a whimpering hen?

 If there is anything to be said
In a verse about X, Y and Z,
Let us trust with the mission
This old mathematician,
Who carries them all in his head.